FRIGHTFULLY FUN
Halloween
RECIPES

Publications International, Ltd.
Favorite Brand Name Recipes at www.fbnr.com

Photography on pages 9, 11, 13, 21, 23, 29, 47, 61, 73 and 79 by Sanders Studios, Inc.
Photographer: Kathy Sanders
Photographer's Assistant: Scott Olson
Prop Stylist: Patty Higgins
Food Stylists: Kim Hartman, Mary-Helen Steindler
Assistant Food Stylist: Kim First

Pictured on the front cover *(clockwise from top left):* Jack-O'-Lantern *(page 64);* Brrrrownie Cats *(page 63)* and Sugar & Spice Jack-O'-Lantern Cookies *(page 56);* Halloween Chicken Pizza Masks *(page 16);* Skeleton Cookies *(page 88).*
Pictured on the back cover *(clockwise from top left):* Skull & Cross Bones *(page 72),* Mummy Dogs *(page 8)* and Macho Monster Cake *(page 86).*

ISBN-13: 978-1-4127-5482-8
ISBN-10: 1-4127-5482-8

Manufactured in China.

8 7 6 5 4 3 2 1

Microwave Cooking: Microwave ovens vary in wattage. Use the cooking times as guidelines and check for doneness before adding more time.

Preparation/Cooking Times: Preparation times are based on the approximate amount of time required to assemble the recipe before cooking, baking, chilling or serving. These times include preparation steps such as measuring, chopping and mixing. The fact that some preparations and cooking can be done simultaneously is taken into account. Preparation of optional ingredients and serving suggestions is not included.

FRIGHTFULLY FUN
Halloween
RECIPES

Happy Halloween!

Critter Cubes

Keep drinks cold with ice cubes that show Halloween spirit! Fill an ice cube tray half full of water; freeze. Place a small gummy creature or piece of candy corn on each ice cube. Cover with water and freeze until completely frozen.

Monster Masks

For any Halloween party, costumes are required but you may want to make festive masks as one of the party activities. Provide a plain mask (either purchased or cut out from poster board or paper plates) for each child and supply paints, markers, colored papers, fabric, yarn and glitter. Stickers are also an easy way to-decorate. Give prizes for the scariest, prettiest or most creative—just be sure every child wins something.

Ghostly Favors

Little monsters will adore these party favors!

◆ Place some small candies in a sandwich bag for the head. Secure the ball tightly with tape.

◆ Drape a napkin over the head and tie a ribbon tightly around the neck.

◆ Draw a face on the ghost.

Make Halloween A Scream!

◆ **Create scary decorations like cobwebs and bats and hang them from the ceiling.**

◆ **Turn down the lights and play a recording of scary sounds to add to the spooky atmosphere.**

◆ **Place a life-sized skeleton inside a closet and decorate with cobwebs. Entice guests into opening the door by hanging a "Do Not Enter" sign on the doorknob.**

Spooky Spiderwebs Game

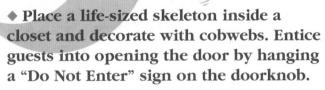

For this game, you'll need a different colored ball of yarn for each team. Before the party begins, tie prizes for each team at the end of each ball of yarn and hide the prize. Then unwind the yarn around a room—around the furniture, under tables, behind the sofa—creating a spiderweb of yarn. When the party starts, pass out the loose ends of yarn to the teams. Have them wind the yarn back up into a ball, following it around the room until they find their prizes.

Haunted Mobile

Cut out Halloween shapes from colored foam or poster board and decorate with wiggle eyes and markers. Along the bottom of the main center piece, punch one hole for each dangling piece. Punch one hole in the tops of the dangling pieces and in the top of the main piece. Attach the dangling pieces to the main piece with different lengths of ribbon.

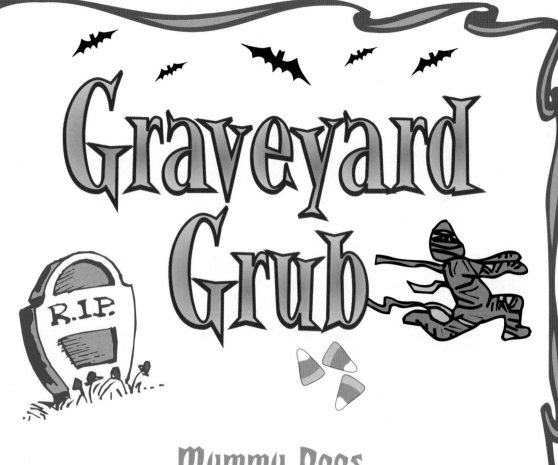

Graveyard Grub

Mummy Dogs

1 package (8 breadsticks or 11 ounces) breadstick dough
1 package (16 ounces) hot dogs
Mustard and poppy seeds

◆ Preheat oven to 375°F. Using 1 dough strip for each, wrap hot dogs to look like mummies, leaving opening for eyes. Place on ungreased baking sheet.

◆ Bake 12 to 15 minutes or until light golden brown.

◆ Place dots of mustard and poppy seeds for eyes.   *Makes 8 servings*

Mini Mummy Dogs: Use 1 package (16 ounces) mini hot dogs instead of regular hot dogs. Cut each breadstick strip into 3 pieces. Cut each piece in half lengthwise. Using 1 strip of dough for each, wrap and bake mini hot dogs as directed above.

Mummy Dogs

Grilled Cheese Jack-O'-Lanterns

3 tablespoons butter or margarine, softened
8 slices bread
4 slices Monterey Jack cheese
4 slices sharp Cheddar cheese

◆ Preheat oven to 350°F. Spread butter on one side of each bread slice. Place bread buttered-side-down on ungreased cookie sheet.

◆ Using small sharp hors d'oeuvre cutter or knife, cut out shapes from 4 bread slices to make jack-o'-lantern face. On remaining bread slices layer 1 slice Monterey Jack and 1 slice Cheddar.

◆ Bake 10 to 12 minutes or until cheese is melted. Remove from oven; place jack-o'-lantern bread slice on sandwiches and serve.

Makes 4 servings

Bat & Spook Pizzas

4 (6-inch) Italian bread shells
⅔ cup pizza or spaghetti sauce
1 package (3½ ounces) pepperoni slices
4 slices (1 ounce each) mozzarella cheese

◆ Preheat oven to 375°F. Place bread shells on ungreased baking sheet.

◆ Spread pizza sauce evenly on bread shells; top evenly with pepperoni slices.

◆ Cut out ghost and bat shapes from cheese slices with cookie cutters; place on pizza sauce.

◆ Bake 10 to 12 minutes or until cheese is melted.

Makes 4 servings

Top to bottom: Grilled Cheese Jack-O'-Lanterns and Potato Bugs
(page 36)

Eyes of Newt

2 cans (2¼ ounces each) sliced black olives, divided
¼ cup chopped roasted red pepper, divided
1 package (8 ounces) cream cheese, softened
1 clove garlic, minced
8 (6- to 7-inch) flour tortillas
16 slices deli roast beef

◆ Reserve 48 olive slices, 48 pieces red pepper and 1 tablespoon cream cheese.

◆ Chop remaining olives. Combine remaining cream cheese, olives, red pepper and garlic in small bowl; mix well.

◆ Spread about 2 tablespoons cream cheese mixture on each tortilla. Top each tortilla with 2 beef slices, overlapping slightly. Roll up tortillas, jelly-roll fashion. Trim off uneven ends of each tortilla; discard. Slice each tortilla roll into 6 (¾-inch) pieces.

◆ Using reserved cream cheese, attach reserved olives and red pepper to make roll-ups look like eyes.   *Makes 4 dozen pieces*

Sloppy Goblins

1 pound lean ground beef
1 cup chopped onion
4 hot dogs, cut into ½-inch pieces
½ cup ketchup
¼ cup chopped dill pickle
¼ cup honey
¼ cup tomato paste
¼ cup prepared mustard
2 teaspoons cider vinegar
1 teaspoon Worcestershire sauce
8 hamburger buns
Decorations: olives, banana peppers, carrot crinkles, red bell pepper, parsley sprigs and pretzel sticks

◆ Cook beef and onion in large skillet over medium heat until beef is brown and onion is tender; drain. Stir in remaining ingredients except buns and decorations. Cook, covered, 5 minutes or until heated through.

◆ Spoon meat mixture onto bottoms of buns; cover with tops of buns. Serve with decorations and let each person create a goblin face. Refrigerate leftovers.
      Makes 8 servings

Top to bottom: Cheesy Bat Biscuits (page 38) and Eyes of Newt

Devilish Delights

1 package (16 ounces) hot roll mix, plus ingredients to prepare mix
1 pound boneless skinless chicken breasts, cut into ¾-inch pieces
2 tablespoons vegetable oil, divided
¾ cup chopped onion
1 clove garlic, minced
1¼ cups sliced zucchini
1 can (8 ounces) peeled diced tomatoes, drained
1 can (4 ounces) sliced mushrooms, drained
1 teaspoon dried basil leaves
½ teaspoon dried oregano leaves
Salt and black pepper
1 cup (4 ounces) shredded mozzarella cheese
1 egg yolk
1 teaspoon water
Red food color

1. Prepare hot roll mix according to package directions. Knead dough on lightly floured surface until smooth, 5 minutes. Cover loosely; let stand 15 minutes.

2. Cook chicken in 1 tablespoon oil in large skillet over medium-high heat 5 to 6 minutes or until no longer pink in center; remove from skillet and set aside. Cook and stir onion and garlic in remaining 1 tablespoon oil in skillet until tender.

3. Stir in zucchini, tomatoes, mushrooms, basil and oregano; bring to a boil. Reduce heat; simmer 5 to 10 minutes or until excess liquid has evaporated. Stir in reserved chicken; cook 1 minute. Remove from heat; season to taste with salt and pepper. Stir in cheese.

4. Preheat oven to 400°F. Grease baking sheets. Roll dough on floured surface to ¼-inch thickness. Cut into equal number of 4-inch circles. Combine scraps and reroll dough if necessary. Place half of circles on prepared baking sheets. Spoon about ¼ cup chicken mixture on half of the circles; top with remaining circles and seal edges with fork. Cut vents to resemble devil; use dough scraps to make horns, eyes, nose and beard.

5. Combine egg yolk and water; brush dough. Add red food color to remaining egg yolk mixture. Brush horns and beard with colored egg mixture.

6. Bake 20 to 25 minutes or until golden. Refrigerate leftovers.
Makes 10 to 12 servings

Top to bottom: Sloppy Goblins (page 12) and Devilish Delight

Halloween Chicken Pizza Masks

1 pound ground chicken
½ cup chopped onion
1 teaspoon salt
1 teaspoon dried oregano
   leaves
½ teaspoon ground black
   pepper
6 English muffins, split
1½ cups prepared pizza
   sauce
1 large green or red bell
   pepper
1 cup (4 ounces)
   shredded Cheddar
   cheese
1 cup (4 ounces)
   shredded mozzarella
   cheese
1 can (2¼ ounces) sliced
   black olives, drained

Heat large skillet over medium-high heat until hot. Add chicken, onion, salt, oregano and black pepper. Cook and stir about 6 minutes or until chicken is no longer pink; set aside. Cover 15½×10½-inch baking pan with foil. Arrange muffins in single layer on prepared pan. Spread 2 tablespoons pizza sauce on each muffin half. Cover generously with chicken mixture, dividing evenly. Cut 12 slivers bell pepper into "smiling" mouth shapes; set aside. Chop remaining bell pepper; sprinkle over mini-pizzas. Combine Cheddar and mozzarella cheeses in small bowl; sprinkle generously over mini-pizzas. Bake at 450°F 12 minutes or until cheese is light brown. Make face on each pizza by using 2 olive slices for "eyes" and 1 pepper shape for "mouth."
Makes 12 mini-pizzas

*Favorite recipe from **National Chicken Council***

A bewitching way to garnish a Halloween dish is with vegetable cutouts! Use a small metal cookie cutter or sharp knife to cut Halloween shapes from bell peppers, carrots, parsnips, squash, eggplant or tomatoes.

Halloween Chicken Pizza Masks

Salsa Macaroni & Cheese

**1 jar (16 ounces) Ragú®
Cheese Creations!®
Double Cheddar
Sauce
1 cup prepared mild salsa
8 ounces elbow macaroni,
cooked and drained**

1. In 2-quart saucepan, heat Ragú Cheese Creations! Sauce over medium heat. Stir in salsa; heat through.

2. Toss with hot macaroni. Serve immediately.   *Makes 4 servings*

Prep Time: 5 minutes
Cook Time: 15 minutes

Peanut Pitas

**1 package (8 ounces)
small pita breads, cut
crosswise in half
16 teaspoons reduced-fat
peanut butter
16 teaspoons strawberry
spreadable fruit
1 large banana, peeled
and thinly sliced
(about 48 slices)**

◆ Spread inside of each pita half with 1 teaspoon each peanut butter and spreadable fruit.

◆ Fill pita halves evenly with banana slices. Serve immediately.
        Makes 8 servings

Honey Bees: Substitute honey for spreadable fruit.

Jolly Jellies: Substitute any flavor jelly for spreadable fruit and thin apple slices for banana slices.

Salsa Macaroni & Cheese

Monster Claws

2 tablespoons flour
1 tablespoon plus
    2 teaspoons cajun
    seasoning, divided
1 pound boneless skinless
    chicken breasts, cut
    lengthwise into
    ¾-inch strips
1½ cups cornflake crumbs
2 tablespoons chopped
    green onion
3 eggs, lightly beaten
1 red, yellow or orange
    bell pepper, cut into
    triangle shapes
Barbecue sauce

◆ Preheat oven to 350°F. Lightly grease baking sheet. Place flour and 2 teaspoons cajun seasoning in large resealable food storage bag. Add chicken and seal. Shake bag to coat chicken.

◆ Combine cornflake crumbs, green onion and remaining 1 tablespoon cajun seasoning in large shallow bowl; mix well.

◆ Place eggs in shallow bowl. Dip each chicken strip into eggs and then into crumb mixture. Place coated chicken strips on prepared baking sheets.

◆ Bake chicken strips 8 to 10 minutes or until chicken is no longer pink in center.

◆ When chicken is cool enough to handle, make ½-inch slit in thinner end. Place bell pepper triangle into slit to form claw nail. Serve claws with barbecue sauce for dipping.

Makes about 30 strips

Make dips, sauces or spreads part of the decor too. Serve them in small plastic cauldrons, skulls or jack-o'-lanterns. For a more natural look, serve them in hollowed out miniature pumpkins, or orange or purple bell peppers.

Monster Claws

Haunted Taco Tarts

1 tablespoon vegetable oil
½ cup chopped onion
½ pound ground turkey
½ teaspoon chili powder
½ teaspoon dried oregano
    leaves
1 clove garlic, minced
¼ teaspoon salt
    Egg Yolk Paint (recipe
    follows)
1 package (15 ounces)
    refrigerated pie crusts
1 egg white
½ cup chopped tomato
½ cup shredded taco-
    flavored cheese

◆ Heat oil in large skillet over medium heat. Add onion and cook until tender. Add turkey; cook until turkey is no longer pink, stirring occasionally. Stir in seasonings; set aside.

◆ Preheat oven to 375°F. Lightly grease baking sheets. Prepare Egg Yolk Paint; set aside.

◆ On lightly floured surface, roll 1 pie crust to 14-inch diameter. Using 3-inch Halloween cookie cutters, cut out pairs of desired shapes. Repeat with second pie crust, rerolling dough if necessary. Place ½ of shapes on prepared baking sheets. Brush edges with egg white. Spoon about 1 tablespoon taco mixture onto each shape. Sprinkle with 1 teaspoon tomato and 1 teaspoon cheese. Top with remaining matching shapes; press edges to seal. Decorate using Egg Yolk Paint.

◆ Bake 10 to 12 minutes or until golden brown.   *Makes 14 tarts*

Egg Yolk Paint

4 egg yolks, divided
4 teaspoons water,
    divided
    Red, yellow, blue and
    green liquid food
    colors

◆ Place 1 egg yolk in each of 4 small bowls. Add 1 teaspoon water and a few drops different food color to each; beat lightly.

Haunted Taco Tarts

Harvest Sticks with Vegetable Dip

2 packages (3 ounces each) cream cheese with chives, softened
1 cup sour cream
⅓ cup finely chopped cucumber
2 tablespoons chopped fresh parsley
2 tablespoons dry minced onion *or* ¼ cup finely chopped fresh onion
1 clove garlic, minced
¼ teaspoon salt
½ teaspoon curry powder (optional)
6 large carrots, peeled
3 medium zucchini

SUPPLIES
Tan raffia

◆ Beat cream cheese in small bowl of until fluffy; blend in sour cream. Stir in cucumber, parsley, onion, garlic and salt. Add curry powder, if desired. Spoon into small serving bowl; cover. Refrigerate 1 hour or until serving time.

◆ Just before serving, cut carrots lengthwise into thin strips; gather into bundles. Tie raffia around bundles to hold in place. Repeat with zucchini.

◆ Place bowl of dip on serving tray; garnish, if desired. Surround with bundles of carrots and zucchini.

Makes about 2 cups dip

These vegetable bundles can be made ahead of time. Cut up the vegetables as directed. Place the carrots in a medium bowl; cover with cold water. Refrigerate until ready to use. Place the zucchini sticks in a small resealable plastic food storage bag and refrigerate until ready to use. Just before serving, gather the vegetables into bundles and tie with raffia as directed.

Left to right: Pumpkin Yeast Rolls (page 26) and Harvest Sticks with Vegetable Dip

Pumpkin Yeast Rolls

16 slivered almonds
¼ teaspoon green food
color
1 package (16 ounces) hot
roll mix
1 to 1¼ teaspoons
pumpkin pie spice
⅔ cup apple cider
⅓ cup warm water
2 tablespoons butter,
softened
1 whole egg, slightly
beaten
1 egg white
2 tablespoons cold water

1. Place almonds in small resealable plastic food storage bag. Add food color; seal bag. Shake bag until almonds are evenly colored. Place almonds on paper-towel-lined plate; let dry.

2. Combine hot roll mix, yeast package from mix and pumpkin pie spice in large bowl; stir to mix well.

3. Combine cider and warm water in small saucepan. Heat over medium heat until cider mixture is hot (120° to 130°F); pour over dry ingredients. Add butter and whole egg; stir until dough pulls away from sides of bowl.

4. Place dough on lightly floured surface; knead until smooth and elastic, about 5 minutes. Let rest 5 minutes. Cut dough into 16 equal pieces; roll each piece into ball. Combine egg white and cold water in small bowl; beat lightly with fork until well blended.

5. Brush egg white mixture evenly onto rolls, covering completely.

6. With sharp knife, lightly score surface of roll, beginning at top center and coming down around sides of rolls, to resemble pumpkin. Insert 1 almond sliver into top of each roll for stem.

7. Lightly grease baking sheet. Place rolls, 2 inches apart, on prepared baking sheet. Cover loosely with towel; let rise in warm place 20 to 30 minutes or until doubled in size. Remove towel.

8. Preheat oven to 375°F. Bake 15 to 20 minutes or until golden brown. *Makes 16 rolls*

Individual Mashed Potato Ghosts

5 cups mashed Idaho Potatoes
Waxed paper
½ cup small black olives

1. Cut ghost shapes out of waxed paper.

2. Place templates on serving dish or cookie sheet. Use rubber spatula to mold ½ to 1 cup potatoes into each ghost shape.

3. Slice olives to create circular shapes to be used for eyes and mouth.   *Makes 4 to 6 servings*

Note: To warm Mashed Potato Ghosts, microwave on HIGH 2 to 4 minutes on microwavable plate. If using oven, place potatoes on cookie sheet and re-heat at 350°F, loosely covered with foil, 7 to 8 minutes or until heated through.

*Favorite recipe from **Idaho Potato Commission***

Western Wagon Wheels

1 pound lean ground beef or ground turkey
2 cups wagon wheel pasta, uncooked
1 can (14½ ounces) stewed tomatoes
1½ cups water
1 box (10 ounces) BIRDS EYE® frozen Sweet Corn
½ cup barbecue sauce
Salt and pepper to taste

◆ In large skillet, cook beef over medium heat 5 minutes or until well browned.

◆ Stir in pasta, tomatoes, water, corn and barbecue sauce; bring to a boil.

◆ Reduce heat to low; cover and simmer 15 to 20 minutes or until pasta is tender, stirring occasionally. Season with salt and pepper.   *Makes 4 servings*

Prep Time: 5 minutes
Cook Time: 25 minutes

Serving Suggestion: Serve with corn bread or corn muffins.

Bewitching Bites

Spider Web Dip

Spooky Tortilla Chips (page 30)
1 package (8 ounces) cream cheese, softened
1 jar (8 ounces) prepared salsa
½ cup prepared guacamole
2 tablespoons sour cream

◆ Prepare Spooky Tortilla Chips; set aside.

◆ Place cream cheese and salsa in blender or food processor container; blend until almost smooth.

continued on page 30

Spider Web Dip

Spider Web Dip, continued

◆ Spread cream cheese mixture on round serving dish or pie plate; smooth guacamole over top, leaving ½-inch border. Place sour cream in small resealable plastic food storage bag; seal bag. Cut off tiny corner of bag; pipe sour cream in circles over guacamole. Run tip of knife through sour cream to make "spider web." Serve with Spooky Tortilla Chips.

Makes 8 to 10 servings

Spooky Tortilla Chips

3 packages (12 ounces each) 8-inch plain or flavored flour tortillas
Salt to taste

◆ Preheat oven to 350°F. Spray baking sheet with olive oil nonstick cooking spray.

◆ Using 3-inch Halloween cookie cutters, cut tortillas, one at a time, into shapes. Discard scraps.

◆ Lightly spray tortilla shapes with cooking spray. Place on prepared baking sheet and sprinkle with salt.

◆ Bake 5 to 7 minutes or until edges begin to brown. Remove to wire rack to cool completely.

Makes about 90 chips

Witches' Brew

2 cups apple cider
1½ to 2 cups vanilla ice cream
2 tablespoons honey
½ teaspoon ground cinnamon
¼ teaspoon ground nutmeg

Process cider, ice cream, honey, cinnamon and nutmeg in food processor or blender until smooth. Pour into glasses and sprinkle with additional nutmeg. Serve immediately.

Makes 4 (6-ounce) servings

Prep Time: 10 minutes

Serving Suggestion: Add a few drops of desired food coloring to ingredients in food processor to make a scary brew.

Lighten Up: To reduce fat, replace vanilla ice cream with reduced-fat or fat-free ice cream or frozen yogurt.

Witches' Brew

Creepy Hands

8 cups popped popcorn
1 cup pumpkin seeds, cleaned and patted dry
⅓ cup butter, melted
1 tablespoon Worcestershire sauce
½ teaspoon garlic salt
½ teaspoon seasoned salt
Candy corn

SUPPLIES
6 clear industrial food handler's gloves
Orange and/or black ribbon
6 plastic spider rings

◆ Preheat oven to 300°F. Place popcorn in single layer in 15×10×1-inch jelly-roll pan; sprinkle with pumpkin seeds.

◆ Mix butter, Worcestershire and salts in small bowl. Pour over popcorn; toss to coat.

◆ Bake 30 minutes, stirring after 15 minutes. Cool completely in pan on wire rack.

◆ Place candy corn in end of each glove finger for fingernail; pack glove tightly with popcorn mixture. Close bag tightly at wrist; tie with ribbon. Place ring on 1 finger of each hand.

Makes 6 servings

Monster Eyes

1 container (8 ounces) plain soft cream cheese
6 miniature bagels, split and toasted
6 midget sweet pickles
Red decorating icing

◆ Spread cream cheese evenly onto toasted bagels, leaving center holes in bagels unfrosted.

◆ Cut pickles crosswise in half; insert, cut sides up, into bagel holes. Use icing to add "veins" and "pupils" to eyes as shown.

Makes 12 appetizer servings

Arrange a "boo-tiful" buffet table. Roll up utensils in a festive napkin and use a Halloween cookie cutter as a napkin ring. To keep utensils in easy reach, set them in a black plastic cauldron placed near the plates.

Clockwise from top left: Chocolate Spiders (page 90), Monster Eyes, Doughnut Hole Spider (page 90) and Creepy Hand

Jack-O'-Lantern Cheese Ball

2 cups (8 ounces) shredded Cheddar cheese
4 ounces cream cheese, softened
¼ cup solid pack pumpkin
¼ cup pineapple preserves
¼ teaspoon ground allspice
¼ teaspoon ground nutmeg
1 pretzel rod, broken in half
Dark rye bread, red pepper and black olive slices
Assorted crackers

◆ Beat cheeses, pumpkin, preserves and spices in medium bowl until smooth. Cover; refrigerate 2 to 3 hours or until cheese is firm enough to shape.

◆ Shape mixture into round pumpkin; place on serving plate. Using knife, score vertical lines down pumpkin. Place pretzel rod in top for stem.

◆ Cut bread into triangles for eyes. Decorate as shown.

◆ Cover loosely; chill until serving time. Serve with crackers.
Makes 16 to 18 servings

Grizzly Gorp

2 cups TEDDY GRAHAM BEARWICH'S® Graham Sandwiches, any flavor
1 cup miniature marshmallows
1 cup dry roasted peanuts
½ cup seedless raisins

In large bowl, combine graham sandwiches, marshmallows, peanuts and raisins. Store in airtight container.
Makes 4½ cups

For a traditional costume party, complete with vampires, ghosts and goblins, make a haunted house or coffin invitation. First fold a piece of black paper in half. Cut out a house or coffin shape without cutting the fold on the left side. Next cut out a ghost or mummy shape from white paper to fit inside the house or coffin. Write the party information on the ghost or mummy.

Jack-O'-Lantern Cheese Ball

Hot Cocoa with Floating Eyeballs

16 large marshmallows
   Black licorice candies
2 quarts milk
1 cup chocolate-flavored
   drink mix
1 cup mint-flavored
   semisweet chocolate
   chips

SUPPLIES
16 lollipop sticks

◆ Make slit in center of each marshmallow; insert licorice candy into slit. Insert lollipop stick into center of bottom of each eyeball; set aside.

◆ Combine milk and drink mix in medium saucepan. Stir in chocolate chips. Cook over medium heat, stirring occasionally, until chips are melted and milk is heated through.

◆ Place 2 eyeballs in each mug; fill mug with hot cocoa. Serve immediately.   *Makes 8 servings*

Potato Bugs

1 package (16 ounces)
   shredded potato
   nuggets
6 pieces uncooked
   spaghetti, broken into
   thirds
1 carrot, cut into 1½-inch
   strips
   Sour cream, black olive
   slices, ketchup and
   broccoli pieces

◆ Preheat oven to 450°F. Lightly grease baking sheets.

◆ Spread potato nuggets on baking sheets. Bake 7 minutes. Loosen nuggets from baking sheets with metal spatula.

◆ Thread 3 potato nuggets onto 1 spaghetti piece. Bake 5 minutes.

◆ Carefully push carrot strips into sides of each nugget for legs. Using sour cream to attach vegetables, decorate faces as shown in photo on page 11.
    Makes about 15 servings

Clockwise from top left: Chocolate-Dipped Caramel Apples (page 63), Hot Cocoa with Floating Eyeballs and Tombstone Place Cards (page 71)

Trick or Treats

12 cups popped corn
1 pound bacon, fried
    crisp, drained and
    broken into 1-inch
    pieces
1 can (12 ounces) mixed
    nuts, toasted
½ cup sunflower seeds,
    toasted
4 tablespoons butter or
    margarine, melted
    and divided
3 tablespoons grated
    Parmesan cheese,
    divided

Combine popped corn, bacon, nuts and sunflower seeds in large bowl. Drizzle mixture with 2 tablespoons butter. Sprinkle with 4½ teaspoons cheese; toss. Repeat with remaining 2 tablespoons butter and 4½ teaspoons cheese. Serve warm.

Makes 12 (1-cup) servings

Prep Time: 30 minutes

Cook's Note: For a quick and easy way to toast sunflower seeds, use the stove-top method. Spread the seeds in a large dry skillet. Heat over medium-low heat, stirring the seeds or shaking the pan frequently, about 4 to 6 minutes or until the seeds turn golden.

Cheesy Bat Biscuits

1 can (16 ounces)
    jumbo refrigerated
    buttermilk biscuits
3 tablespoons butter,
    melted and divided
¼ cup grated Parmesan
    cheese
1 teaspoon dried parsley
    flakes
1 teaspoon dried basil
    leaves

◆ Preheat oven to 350°F.

◆ Flatten each biscuit into shape until just large enough to fit 3-inch bat cookie cutter. Cut out bat shape; discard scraps. Place biscuits on baking sheet. Lightly score biscuits to outline bat wings; poke holes for eyes with toothpick. Brush biscuits with 1 tablespoon butter. Bake 7 minutes.

◆ Meanwhile, combine cheese, remaining 2 tablespoons butter, parsley and basil in small bowl.

◆ Turn biscuits on end and split into halves with forks. Spread 1 teaspoon cheese mixture on bottom half of each biscuit; replace biscuit top. Bake 3 minutes or until biscuits are golden.   *Makes 8 servings*

Trick or Treats

Magic Potion

Creepy Crawler Ice Ring
(recipe follows)
1 cup boiling water
2 packages (4-serving size each) lime-flavored gelatin
3 cups cold water
1½ quarts carbonated lemon-lime beverage, chilled
½ cup superfine sugar
Gummy worms (optional)

◆ One day ahead, prepare Creepy Crawler Ice Ring.

◆ Pour boiling water over gelatin in heatproof punch bowl; stir until gelatin dissolves. Stir in cold water. Add lemon-lime beverage and sugar; stir well (mixture will foam for several minutes).

◆ Unmold ice ring by dipping bottom of mold briefly into hot water. Float ice ring in punch. Serve cups of punch garnished with gummy worms, if desired.

Makes about 10 servings

Creepy Crawler Ice Ring

1 cup gummy worms or other creepy crawler candy
1 quart lemon-lime thirst quencher beverage

◆ Arrange gummy worms in bottom of 5-cup ring mold; fill mold with thirst quencher beverage. Freeze until solid, 8 hours or overnight.

Change this Magic Potion from creepy to cute with just a few simple substitutions. For the punch, use orange-flavored gelatin instead of lime. For the ice ring, use candy corn and candy pumpkins instead of gummy worms.

Eyeballs

12 hard-cooked eggs
1 can (4½ ounces) deviled ham
⅓ cup mayonnaise
4 teaspoons prepared mustard
¼ cup drained sweet pickle relish
12 pimiento-stuffed olives, halved

◆ Cut eggs lengthwise into halves. Remove yolks; place in small bowl. Mash egg yolks with fork; mix in deviled ham, mayonnaise, mustard and pickle relish. Season to taste with salt and pepper.

◆ Spoon filling into egg halves. Garnish with olive halves to make "eyeballs."

◆ To make extra scary bloodshot "eyeballs," spoon ketchup into small resealable plastic food storage bag. Cut off very tiny corner of bag; drizzle over eggs.

Makes 12 servings

Prep Time: 25 minutes

Note: To save time, use leftover ketchup packets to drizzle over eggs to make bloodshot "eyeballs."

Cinnamon Apple Chips

2 cups unsweetened apple juice
1 cinnamon stick
2 Washington Red Delicious apples

1. In large skillet or saucepan, combine apple juice and cinnamon stick; bring to a low boil while preparing apples.

2. Slice off ½ inch from top and bottom of apples and discard. Stand apples on either cut end; cut crosswise into ⅛-inch-thick slices, rotating apple to cut even slices.

3. Drop slices into boiling juice; cook 4 to 5 minutes or until slices appear translucent and lightly golden. Meanwhile, preheat oven to 250°F.

4. Remove apple slices from juice and pat dry. Arrange slices on wire racks, being sure none overlap. Place racks on middle shelf in oven; bake 30 to 40 minutes until slices are lightly browned and almost dry to touch. Cool completely before storing in airtight container.

Makes about 40 chips

*Favorite recipe from **Washington Apple Commission***

Eyeballs

Trick-or-Treat Punch

Green food color
1 envelope (4 ounces)
 orange-flavored
 presweetened drink
 mix
1 can (12 ounces)
 frozen lemonade
 concentrate, thawed
1 bottle (2 liters) ginger
 ale*

SUPPLIES
 1 new plastic household
 glove

*For an adult party, substitute 2 bottles (750 ml each) champagne for ginger ale, if desired.

◆ One day ahead, fill pitcher with 3 cups water; color with green food color. Pour into glove; tightly secure top of glove with twist tie. Cover baking sheet with paper towels; place glove on prepared baking sheet. Use inverted custard cup to elevate tied end of glove to prevent leaking. Freeze overnight.

◆ When ready to serve, combine drink mix, lemonade concentrate and 4 cups water in large bowl; stir until drink mix is dissolved and mixture is well blended. Pour into punch bowl; add ginger ale.

◆ Cut glove away from ice; float frozen hand in punch.
Makes 16 (6-ounce) servings and 1 ice hand

Make this punch a ghoulish centerpiece. Serve the punch, with the ice hand, in a large plastic black cauldron. Then surround it with an array of spooky treats.

Top to bottom: Trick-or-Treat Punch and Orange Jack-O'-Lanterns (page 82)

Tricky Treats

Ghost on a Stick

4 medium pears, stems removed
9 squares (2 ounces each) almond bark
   Mini chocolate chips

SUPPLIES
   4 wooden craft sticks

◆ Line baking sheet with waxed paper. Insert sticks into stem ends of pears. Melt bark according to package directions. Dip pear into bark, spooning over top to coat evenly. Remove excess by scraping pear bottom across rim of measuring cup. Place on baking cup; let set 1 minute. Decorate with chocolate chips. Repeat with remaining pears. Place spoonful of extra almond bark at bottom of pears for ghost tails. Refrigerate until firm.   *Makes 4 servings*

Left to right: Monster Munch (page 53) and Ghost on a Stick

Little Devils

1 package (1 pound 2 ounces) carrot cake mix
½ cup solid-pack pumpkin
⅓ cup vegetable oil
3 eggs
1 container (16 ounces) cream cheese frosting
Assorted Halloween candies, jelly beans, chocolate candies and nuts

◆ Preheat oven to 350°F. Prepare cake mix according to package directions, using water as directed on package, pumpkin, oil and eggs. Spoon batter into 18 paper-lined muffin cups. Bake 20 minutes or until toothpick inserted in centers of cupcakes comes out clean. Cool in pans on wire rack 5 minutes; remove and cool completely.

◆ Frost cupcakes with frosting; let each goblin guest decorate his own with assorted candies.

Makes 18 cupcakes

Make-Ahead Time: up to 3 days in refrigerator or up to 1 month in freezer before serving
Final Prep Time: 20 minutes

Spiders

1 (3-inch) oatmeal cookie
1 tablespoon Fluffy White Frosting (page 68)
1 small black jelly bean
1 large black jelly bean
1 black licorice whip
2 red candy-coated licorice pieces

Frost oatmeal cookie with Fluffy White Frosting. Arrange jelly beans on cookies to make spider head and body. Cut 6 to 8 licorice whip pieces (about 1½ inches long); curve and position for legs. Add red candy antennae to head.

Makes 1 cookie

If weather permits, a treasure hunt in the back yard is a great party activity. Some fun prizes to hide are decorated pencils and erasers, stickers, pennies, wrapped candies and small toys, such as spider rings.

Little Devils

Full-Moon Pumpkin Cheesecake

Gingersnap Cookie Crust (page 52)
4 packages (8 ounces each) cream cheese, softened
½ cup sugar
6 eggs
1 cup sour cream
1 cup solid pack pumpkin
2 tablespoons all-purpose flour
2 teaspoons ground cinnamon
½ teaspoon ground ginger
½ teaspoon ground allspice
3 ounces semisweet chocolate, melted
1 recipe Black Cat Fudge (page 52)

◆ Prepare Gingersnap Cookie Crust; set aside.

◆ *Increase oven temperature to 425°F.* Beat cream cheese in large bowl until fluffy; beat in sugar and eggs, one at a time. Add sour cream, pumpkin, flour and spices; beat well. Pour 2 cups batter into small bowl; stir in chocolate.

◆ Pour remaining batter into prepared crust. Spoon chocolate batter in large swirls over batter in pan; draw knife through mixture to marbleize.

◆ Bake 15 minutes. *Reduce oven temperature to 300°F.* Bake 45 minutes (center of cheesecake will not be set). Turn oven off; let cheesecake stand in oven with door slightly ajar 1 hour. Cool to room temperature in pan on wire rack. Cover; refrigerate in pan overnight.

◆ Prepare Black Cat Fudge; do not cut. Using diagram as guide, cut out witch shape. Score with knife. Cut small star shapes from scraps with cutter or sharp knife.

◆ Remove side of pan from cheesecake; place cheesecake on serving plate. Carefully position witch on cheesecake as shown in photo. Position stars as shown.
Makes 1 (9-inch) cheesecake (about 15 servings)
continued on page 52

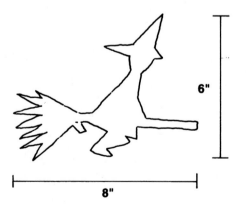

Full-Moon Pumpkin Cheesecake

Full-Moon Pumpkin Cheesecake, continued

Gingersnap Cookie Crust

1 cup gingersnap cookie crumbs
½ cup chopped pecans
¼ cup butter or margarine, melted

◆ Preheat oven to 350F. Combine cookie crumbs and nuts in small bowl. Mix in butter.

◆ Press mixture on bottom and 1-inch up side of 9-inch springform pan.

◆ Bake 8 minutes; cool.

Black Cat Fudge

8 ounces semisweet chocolate, coarsely chopped
¼ cup butter or margarine
⅓ cup light corn syrup
¼ cup whipping cream
1 teaspoon vanilla
¼ teaspoon salt
4½ cups powdered sugar, sifted
30 vanilla milk chips

◆ Line 11×7-inch pan with foil, extending foil beyond edges of pan; grease foil.

◆ Melt chocolate and butter in medium saucepan over low heat; stir in corn syrup, cream, vanilla and salt. Remove from heat; stir in sugar until smooth. Spread in prepared pan. Chill until firm, 1 to 2 hours.

◆ Remove fudge from pan using foil; peel off foil. Following diagram, cut out cats. Clean knife often to prevent sticking. Place 2 vanilla chips on each for eyes. Score feet for claws. Cover and chill.   *Makes about 1½ pounds (12 to 15 cats)*

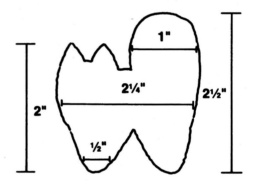

Monster Munch

6 squares (2 ounces each) almond bark, divided
1½ cups pretzel sticks
Orange food coloring
2 cups graham cereal
¾ cup Halloween colored candy-coated chocolate pieces
¾ cup miniature marshmallows
½ cup chocolate sprinkles

◆ Place 1½ squares almond bark in small microwavable bowl. Microwave at MEDIUM (50% power) 1 minute; stir. Repeat steps as necessary, stirring at 15-second intervals, until completely melted.

◆ Place pretzel sticks in large bowl. Add melted almond bark and stir until all pieces are coated. Spread coated pretzel sticks out on waxed paper, separating pieces; let set.

◆ Place remaining 4½ squares almond bark in medium microwavable bowl. Microwave at MEDIUM (50% power) 1 minute; stir. Repeat steps as necessary, stirring at 15-second intervals, until completely melted. Stir in food coloring until almond bark is bright orange.

◆ Place cereal in large bowl. Add half of orange-colored almond bark and stir until cereal is evenly coated. Add chocolate pieces, marshmallows and remaining almond bark; stir until mix is evenly coated. Stir in pretzel sticks.

◆ Break mix into small clusters and spread out on waxed paper. Immediately sprinkle clusters with chocolate sprinkles; let set.
Makes about 5 cups snack mix

Serve this sweet snack mix in a homemade candy corn bowl! Start with any size clean terra cotta flower pot. Paint the bottom white, the middle orange and the top yellow. To use for serving, plug the bottom hole with aluminum foil and fill with candy, nuts or snack mix.

Boo the Ghost

1 (13×9-inch) cake,
    completely cooled
2 cups Light & Fluffy
    Frosting (recipe
    follows)
2 black licorice drops or
    jelly beans

SUPPLIES
1 (19×13) cake board, cut
    in half crosswise and
    covered
Plastic spiders
    (optional)

◆ If cake top is rounded, trim horizontally with long serrated knife. Trim sides of cake.

◆ Using photo as guide, draw ghost outline on 13×9-inch piece of waxed paper. Cut pattern out and place on cake. Cut out ghost. Place on prepared cake board.

◆ Prepare Light & Fluffy Frosting. Frost ghost, swirling frosting. Arrange licorice drops for eyes and spiders as shown in photo.
Makes 12 to 14 servings

Light & Fluffy Frosting

⅔ cup sugar
2 egg whites*
5 teaspoons light corn
    syrup
Dash salt
1 teaspoon vanilla

*Use only Grade A clean, uncracked eggs.

Combine sugar, egg whites, corn syrup and salt in top of double boiler. Set over boiling water. Beat constantly until stiff peaks form, about 7 minutes. Remove from heat; beat in vanilla.

Haunted Hint

Cake boards are made of sturdy cardboard and are available in various sizes and shapes in craft and kitchenware stores. They can be covered with foil, paper doilies or plastic wrap. If a cake is very heavy, stack two cake boards together before covering for additional support.

Boo the Ghost

Sugar & Spice Jack-O'-Lantern Cookies

2⅓ cups all-purpose flour
2 teaspoons ground cinnamon
1½ teaspoons baking powder
1½ teaspoons ground ginger
½ teaspoon salt
¼ teaspoon nutmeg
¾ cup (1½ sticks) butter, softened
½ cup packed brown sugar
½ cup molasses
1 egg
Assorted Halloween cookie decorations, such as orange and black frostings and sprinkles

◆ Combine flour, cinnamon, baking powder, ginger, salt and nutmeg in medium bowl.

◆ Beat butter and sugar in large bowl with electric mixer at medium speed until light and fluffy. Add molasses and egg; beat until well blended. Gradually beat in flour mixture until just combined.

◆ Shape dough into 2 balls; press into 2-inch-thick discs. Wrap in plastic wrap; refrigerate at least 1 hour or until firm.

◆ Preheat oven to 350°F.

◆ Roll out dough on lightly floured surface to ¼-inch thickness. Cut out cookies with jack-o'-lantern cookie cutters or other shapes. Place cutouts on ungreased cookie sheets.

◆ Bake about 12 to 14 minutes or until centers are firm. Cool on cookie sheets 1 minute. Remove to wire racks; cool completely. Frost and decorate cookies as desired.

Makes 2 to 3 dozen cookies

Haunted Hint

Give your guests goosebumps when you present "A Ghost's Tale." Turn off all the lights and then read a spine-tingling story by candlelight or flashlight. Have another adult or older child stand behind the party guests and make eerie sound effects to go with the story.

Sugar & Spice Jack-O'-Lantern Cookies and Brrrrownie Cats (page 63)

Candy Corn Cookies

Butter Cookie dough
(recipe follows)
Cookie Glaze (recipe
follows)
Yellow and orange food
colors

◆ Preheat oven to 350°F.

◆ Roll dough on floured surface to ¼-inch thickness. Using photo as guide, cut out 3-inch candy corn shapes. Place cutouts on ungreased cookie sheets.

◆ Bake 8 to 10 minutes or until edges are lightly browned. Remove to wire racks to cool completely. Prepare Cookie Glaze.

◆ Place racks over waxed-paper-covered baking sheets. Divide Cookie Glaze into thirds; place in separate small bowls. Color ⅓ of glaze with yellow food color and ⅓ with orange food color. Leave remaining glaze white. Spoon different colored glazes over cookies to resemble "candy corn" as shown in photo. Let stand until glaze is set.

Makes about 2 dozen cookies

Butter Cookie Dough

¾ cup butter, softened
¼ cup granulated sugar
¼ cup packed light brown
    sugar
1 egg yolk
1¾ cups all-purpose flour
¾ teaspoon baking
    powder
⅛ teaspoon salt

◆ Combine butter, granulated sugar, brown sugar and egg yolk in medium bowl. Add flour, baking powder and salt; mix well.

◆ Cover; refrigerate about 4 hours or until firm.

Cookie Glaze: Combine 4 cups powdered sugar and 4 tablespoons milk in small bowl. Add 1 to 2 tablespoons more milk as needed to make medium-thick, pourable glaze.

Bat Cookies: Omit yellow and orange food colors. Prepare recipe as directed except use bat cookie cutter to cut out cookies. Bake as directed. Color glaze with black paste food color; spoon over cookies. Decorate with assorted candies as shown in photo.

*Top to bottom: Bat Cookies and
Candy Corn Cookies*

Scarecrow Cupcakes

1¼ cups all-purpose flour
¾ teaspoon baking powder
½ teaspoon baking soda
¼ teaspoon salt
¾ teaspoon ground cinnamon
⅛ teaspoon ground cloves
⅛ teaspoon ground nutmeg
⅛ teaspoon ground allspice
¾ cup heavy cream
2 tablespoons molasses
¼ cup butter, softened
¼ cup sugar
¼ cup packed brown sugar
2 eggs
½ teaspoon vanilla extract
¾ cup sweetened shredded coconut
Maple Buttercream Frosting (page 62)
Toasted coconut, chow mein noodles, shredded wheat cereal, candy corn, candy-coated chocolate pieces, gumdrops and decorator gel

◆ Preheat oven to 350°F. Line 18 (2¾-inch) muffin cups with paper baking liners. Mix flour, baking powder, baking soda, salt and spices in medium bowl; set aside. Mix cream and molasses in small bowl; set aside.

◆ Beat butter in large bowl until creamy. Add sugars; beat until light and fluffy. Add eggs, one at a time, beating well after each addition. Blend in vanilla.

◆ Add flour mixture alternately with cream mixture, beating well after each addition. Stir in coconut; spoon batter into prepared muffin cups, filling about half full.

◆ Bake 20 to 25 minutes or until wooden toothpick inserted in centers comes out clean. Cool in pan on wire rack 10 minutes. Remove cupcakes to racks; cool.

◆ Prepare Maple Buttercream Frosting. Frost cupcakes and decorate to make scarecrow faces as shown in photo.

Makes 18 servings
continued on page 62

Scarecrow Cupcakes, continued

Maple Buttercream Frosting

**2 tablespoons butter,
softened
2 tablespoons maple or
pancake syrup
1½ cups powdered sugar**

◆ Beat butter and syrup in
medium bowl until blended.
Gradually beat in powdered
sugar until smooth.

Makes about 1½ cups

To make a gumdrop hat, roll out a
large gumdrop on a generously sugared
surface. Cut 1 rounded piece to look
like the top of the hat and 1 straight
piece to look the like the brim of the
hat as shown in the photo. Overlap the
pieces to make the hat; pipe decorator
gel over the seam for the hat band.

Boo Bites

**¼ cup (½ stick) butter or
margarine
30 large marshmallows
or 3 cups miniature
marshmallows
¼ cup light corn syrup
½ cup REESE'S® Creamy
Peanut Butter
⅓ cup HERSHEY'S Semi-
Sweet Chocolate
Chips
4½ cups crisp rice cereal**

Line cookie sheet with wax
paper.

Melt butter in large
saucepan over low heat. Add
marshmallows. Cook, stirring
constantly, until marshmallows
are melted. Remove from heat.
Add corn syrup; stir until well
blended. Add peanut butter and
chocolate chips; stir until chips
are melted and mixture is well
blended.

Add cereal; stir until evenly
coated. Cool slightly. With wet
hands, shape mixture into
1½-inch balls; place balls on
prepared cookie sheet. Cool
completely. Store in tightly
covered container in cool, dry
place.

Makes about 4 dozen pieces

Chocolate-Dipped Caramel Apples

1 package (14 ounces)
    caramels
1 tablespoon water
6 medium apples
4 ounces milk or
    semisweet chocolate
    confectionary
    coating, coarsely
    chopped
White decorating icing
Candy corn, gummy
    worms and assorted
    candies
6 wooden craft sticks

◆ Cover baking sheet with waxed paper. Unwrap caramels. Combine caramels and water in medium saucepan; cook over medium heat, stirring constantly, until caramels are melted.

◆ Rinse and thoroughly dry apples; insert wooden sticks into stem ends. Dip apples, 1 at a time, into caramel mixture, coating completely. Remove excess caramel by scraping apple bottom across rim of saucepan. Place on waxed paper.

◆ Place confectionary coating in small saucepan. Cook over low heat, stirring frequently, until chocolate is melted. Dip apples halfway into chocolate. Return to waxed paper.

◆ Use icing to write names on apples. Use small amount of additional icing to secure desired decorations on apples. Chill until firm.   *Makes 6 servings*

Brrrrownie Cats

1 cup (2 sticks) unsalted
    butter
4 ounces unsweetened
    chocolate
1½ cups sugar
3 eggs
1 cup all-purpose flour
¼ teaspoon salt
    Black frosting, sprinkles
    and decors

◆ Preheat oven to 350°F. Grease 13×9-inch baking pan. Melt butter and chocolate in top of double boiler, stirring occasionally.

◆ Transfer butter mixture to large bowl. Stir in sugar until well blended. Beat in eggs, one at a time. Stir in flour and salt. Spread batter into prepared pan. Bake 20 to 25 minutes or just until firm. Cool completely in pan on wire rack.

◆ Cut brownies into cat shapes using Halloween cookie cutters. Decorate as desired.
    Makes about 2 dozen brownies

Jack-O'-Lantern

2 (10-inch) Bundt cakes
2 recipes Buttercream Frosting (recipe follows)
Orange, green and brown paste food colors
Candy corn

SUPPLIES
2 (10-inch) round cake boards, stacked and covered, or large plate
1 (6-ounce) paper cup or ice cream wafer cone
Pastry bag and medium writing tip

◆ Prepare 2 recipes Buttercream Frosting. Tint 4½ cups frosting orange, ½ cup dark green and ¼ cup dark brown. To tint frosting, add small amount of desired paste color with toothpick; stir well. Slowly add more color until frosting is desired shade.

◆ Trim flat sides of cakes. Place one cake on prepared cake board, flat-side up. Frost top of cake with some of the orange frosting. Place second cake, flat-side down, over frosting.

◆ Frost entire cake with orange frosting.

◆ Hold cup over fingers of one hand. Using other hand, frost cup with green frosting. Place upside-down in center of cake to form stem. Touch up frosting, if needed.

◆ Using writing tip and brown frosting, pipe eyes and mouth. Arrange candy corn for teeth as shown in photo. Before serving, remove stem. Slice and serve top cake first, then bottom.

Makes 36 to 40 servings

Buttercream Frosting

6 cups powdered sugar, sifted and divided
¾ cup butter, softened
¼ cup shortening
6 to 8 tablespoons milk, divided
1 teaspoon vanilla

◆ Combine 3 cups powdered sugar, butter, shortening, 4 tablespoons milk and vanilla in large bowl. Beat with electric mixer until smooth. Add remaining powdered sugar; beat until light and fluffy, adding more milk, 1 tablespoon at a time, as needed for good spreading consistency.

Makes about 3½ cups

Chocolate Spider Web Cake

1⅔ cups all-purpose flour
1½ cups sugar
½ cup HERSHEY'S Cocoa
1½ teaspoons baking soda
1 teaspoon salt
½ teaspoon baking powder
2 eggs
1½ cups buttermilk or sour milk*
½ cup shortening (do not use butter, margarine, spread or oil)
1 teaspoon vanilla extract
One-Bowl Buttercream Frosting (recipe follows)
Spider Web (page 68)

*To sour milk: Use 4½ teaspoons white vinegar plus milk to equal 1½ cups.

1. Heat oven to 350°F. Thoroughly grease and flour two 9-inch round baking pans.

2. Combine dry ingredients in large bowl; add eggs, buttermilk, shortening and vanilla. Beat on low speed of mixer 1 minute, scraping bowl constantly. Beat on high speed 3 minutes, scraping bowl occasionally. Pour batter into prepared pans.

3. Bake 30 to 35 minutes or until wooden pick inserted in center comes out clean. Cool 10 minutes; remove from pans to wire racks. Cool completely.

4. Frost with One-Bowl Buttercream Frosting. Immediately pipe or drizzle Spider Web in 4 or 5 circles on top of cake. Using a knife or wooden pick, immediately draw 8 to 10 lines from center to edges of cake at regular intervals to form web. Garnish with a "spider," using a cookie, licorice and other candies.

Makes 12 servings

One-Bowl Buttercream Frosting

6 tablespoons butter or margarine, softened
2⅔ cups powdered sugar
½ cup HERSHEY'S Cocoa
4 to 6 tablespoons milk
1 teaspoon vanilla extract

Beat butter; add powdered sugar and cocoa alternately with milk, beating to spreading consistency. Stir in vanilla.

Makes about 2 cups frosting
continued on page 68

Chocolate Spider Web Cake, continued

Spider Web: Place ½ cup HERSHEY'S Premier White Chips and ½ teaspoon shortening (do not use butter, margarine, spread or oil) in small heavy seal-top plastic bag. Microwave at HIGH (100%) 45 seconds. Squeeze gently. If necessary, microwave an additional 10 to 15 seconds; squeeze until chips are melted. With scissors, make small diagonal cut in bottom corner of bag; squeeze mixture onto cake as directed.

If your party is in the back yard or in the basement, have guests enter at the front door of the house and go through a maze of furniture, cardboard or sheets to get to the entrance of the party. Make the maze creepy with dim lights, terrifying sounds and plenty of cobwebs!

Funny Bug

> 1 (3-inch) oatmeal cookie
> 1 tablespoon Fluffy White Frosting (recipe follows)
> 2 miniature chocolate sandwich cookies
> 1 red gumdrop
> 2 cheese corn curls

Frost oatmeal cookie with Fluffy White Frosting. Arrange sandwich cookies to make eyes. Attach gumdrop mouth and corn curl antennae.   *Makes 1 cookie*

Fluffy White Frosting: Mix 1 (16-ounce) container vanilla frosting and ¾ cup marshmallow creme in medium bowl; mix well. Makes about 2 cups.

Clockwise from top left: Funny Bugs, Spider (page 48), Spooky Ghost Cookies (page 70), Bloodshot Eyeballs (page 74)

Spooky Ghost Cookies

1 recipe Butter Cookie
Dough (page 58)
1 recipe Fluffy White
Frosting (page 68)
½ cup semisweet
chocolate chips
(about 60 chips)

◆ Preheat oven to 350°F. Roll dough on floured surface to ¼-inch thickness. Cut out ghost shapes using 3-inch cookie cutter.

◆ Bake on ungreased cookie sheets 10 to 12 minutes until edges begin to brown. Remove to wire racks; cool completely.

◆ Prepare Fluffy White Frosting. Spread frosting over cookies, swirling to give ghostly appearance. Position 2 chocolate chips on each cookie for eyes.

Makes about 2½ dozen cookies

Magic Dip

1 package (8 ounces)
PHILADELPHIA®
Cream Cheese,
softened
1 cup BAKER'S® Semi-
Sweet Real Chocolate
Chips
½ cup BAKER'S® ANGEL
FLAKE® Coconut,
toasted
½ cup chopped peanuts
Graham crackers

SPREAD cream cheese on bottom of 9-inch microwavable pie plate or quiche dish.

TOP with remaining ingredients.

MICROWAVE on MEDIUM (50% power) 3 to 4 minutes or until warm. Serve with graham crackers. Garnish, if desired.

Makes 6 to 8 servings

Prep Time: 5 minutes
Microwave Time: 4 minutes

Tombstone Place Cards

½ container (16 ounces)
    vanilla frosting
8 (2×1¼-inch) fudge-
    coated graham
    cracker cookies
8 fun-size (2-inch) milk-
    chocolate-covered
    caramel candy bars
½ container (16 ounces)
    chocolate frosting
4 whole graham crackers
Pumpkin candies
½ cup sweetened
    shredded coconut,
    tinted green

SUPPLIES
Pastry bag and small
    writing tip

◆ Spoon vanilla frosting into
pastry bag fitted with writing
tip; use to write names on fudge-
coated graham cracker cookies.

◆ Cover tops of candy bars
with small amount of chocolate
frosting; stand fudge-coated
graham crackers upright on
candy bars to form tombstone
shapes.

◆ Break graham crackers in half
crosswise; spread tops with
chocolate frosting. Position candy
tombstones and pumpkins in
chocolate frosting on graham
crackers; sprinkle with coconut
to resemble grass.

Makes 8 place cards

To tint coconut green, add a few drops
of green food color and ¼ teaspoon
water to a large resealable plastic food
storage bag. Add ½ cup sweetened
shredded coconut. Seal the bag and
shake it until the coconut is evenly
colored.

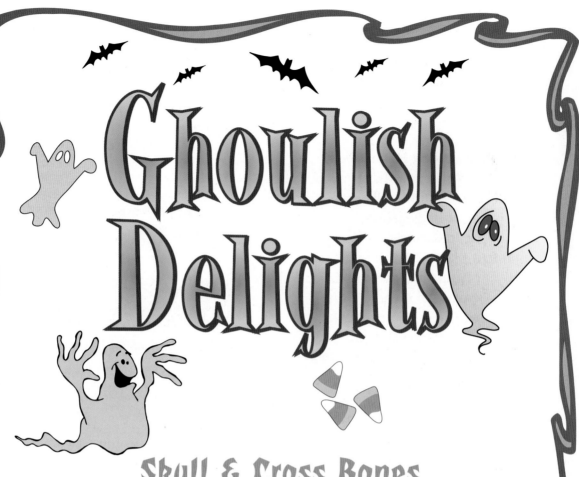

Ghoulish Delights

Skull & Cross Bones

1 package (21.5 ounces) brownie mix, plus ingredients to
   prepare mix
1 egg white
⅛ teaspoon almond extract, optional
¼ cup sugar
   Red and black decorator gels
1 container (16 ounces) prepared chocolate frosting

SUPPLIES
   Pastry bag with medium writing tip

◆ Prepare and bake brownies in 13×9-inch baking pan according to package directions. Cool completely.

◆ Preheat oven to 250°F. Line baking sheet with parchment paper.

continued on page 74

Skull & Cross Bones

Skull & Cross Bones, continued

◆ Beat egg white in large bowl until foamy. Add almond extract, if desired; beat until soft peaks form. Gradually add sugar; beat until stiff peaks form.

◆ Fill pastry bag with egg white mixture. Pipe 24 skull and cross bones shapes onto prepared baking sheet. Bake about 12 minutes or until set. Cool on pan on wire racks. Carefully remove meringues from parchment paper. Decorate with red gel for eyes and black gel for mouths.

◆ Frost brownies and cut into 24 rectangles. Place one meringue on each brownie.

Makes 2 dozen brownies

Get everyone involved in your Halloween party! Have adults or older kids dress up in scary costumes and be camouflaged in the haunted setting. They can pop out at a pre-arranged time for maximum frightfulness.

Bloodshot Eyeballs

2 fudge-covered chocolate sandwich cookies
1 tablespoon Fluffy White Frosting (recipe follows)
2 green jelly beans
Red decorating gel

Frost cookies with Fluffy White Frosting, leaving edge of cookie showing. Press jelly beans into frosting to make pupils of eyes. Decorate with red gel to make eyes look bloodshot.

Makes 2 eyeballs

Fluffy White Frosting: Mix 1 (16-ounce) container vanilla frosting and ¾ cup marshmallow creme in medium bowl; mix well. Makes about 2 cups.

The Big Spider Web

1½ cups all-purpose flour
½ teaspoon baking soda
¾ cup creamy peanut butter
½ cup margarine or butter, softened
1¼ cups firmly packed light brown sugar
2 teaspoons vanilla extract
1 egg
¾ cup milk chocolate chips, divided
½ cup PLANTERS® Dry Roasted Peanuts, chopped
1 cup marshmallow fluff
Assorted candies and gummy creatures

Combine flour and baking soda; set aside.

In large bowl, with electric mixer at medium speed, beat peanut butter, margarine, sugar and vanilla until creamy. Beat in egg until light and fluffy; gradually blend in flour mixture. Stir in ½ cup chocolate chips and chopped peanuts.

Press dough into greased 14-inch pizza pan. Bake at 350°F for 20 to 25 minutes or until done. Cool completely in pan on wire rack. Frost top of cookie with marshmallow fluff to within 1-inch of edge. Melt remaining ¼ cup chocolate chips; drizzle chocolate in circular pattern over marshmallow. Draw knife through marshmallow topping to create web effect. Decorate with assorted candies and gummy creatures. *Makes 16 servings*

Halloween is the perfect time to have a theme party! Choose a theme that has a wide variety of costume options, such as "A Trip to the Zoo," "Under the Sea" or "The Insect World." Make the invitations, food, decorations, and even the games reflect the theme.

Witch Cake

1 package (2-layer size) cake mix, any flavor, plus ingredients to prepare mix
2 containers (16 ounces each) vanilla frosting
Green paste food color
Black decorating gel
Black paste food color
Red licorice whips
1 sugar cone
Assorted candies
Red chewy fruit snack roll-up cutouts

SUPPLIES
1 (15×10-inch) cake board, covered, or large tray
Pastry bag and medium star tip
1 purchased witch's black hat

◆ Preheat oven to 350°F. Grease and flour 13×9-inch baking pan.

◆ Prepare cake according to package directions; pour batter into prepared pan.

◆ Bake 30 to 35 minutes or until wooden toothpick inserted into center comes out clean. Cool in pan on wire rack 10 minutes. Remove from pan to rack; cool.

◆ If cake top is rounded, trim horizontally with long serrated knife. Place cake on prepared cake board. Spread top and sides of cake with 1 container frosting. Transfer about half of remaining container frosting to small bowl; color with green food color.

◆ Using photo as guide, trace outline of witch's head onto frosted cake with toothpick. Fill in face with thin layer of green frosting; outline with decorating gel as shown in photo.

◆ Place remaining frosting in another small bowl; color with black paste food color. Spoon into pastry bag fitted with star tip; pipe frosting around edges of cake.

◆ Cut hat in half lengthwise. Place one half on cake; discard remaining half. Cut licorice into desired lengths. Place around hat to resemble hair as shown in photo.

◆ Place sugar cone on cake for nose. Use candies and fruit snack cutouts to make eyes and mouth.
Makes 12 servings

Coffin Cookies

1 package (18 ounces) refrigerated chocolate cookie dough*
Marshmallow Filling (recipe follows)
Colored sprinkles, sugars and decors
White decorating icing

*If refrigerated chocolate cookie dough is unavailable, add ¼ cup unsweetened cocoa powder to refrigerated sugar cookie dough. Beat in large bowl until well blended.

◆ Draw pattern for coffin on cardboard following diagram; cut out pattern.

◆ Preheat oven to 350°F. Remove dough from wrapper according to package directions. Divide dough into 2 equal sections. Reserve 1 section; cover and refrigerate remaining section.

◆ Roll reserved dough on lightly floured surface to ⅛-inch thickness. Sprinkle with flour to minimize sticking, if necessary.

◆ Place pattern on cookie dough; cut dough around pattern with sharp knife. Repeat as necessary. Place cookies 2 inches apart on ungreased baking sheets. Repeat with remaining dough and scraps.

◆ Bake about 6 minutes or until firm but not browned. Cool on baking sheets 2 minutes. Remove to wire rack; cool completely.

◆ Prepare Marshmallow Filling. Spread half of cookies with 2 teaspoons filling each; top with remaining cookies. Roll cookie sandwich edges in sprinkles.

◆ Decorate as desired.

Makes about 2 dozen sandwich cookies

Marshmallow Filling

1 cup prepared vanilla frosting
¾ cup marshmallow creme

◆ Combine frosting and marshmallow creme in small bowl until well blended.

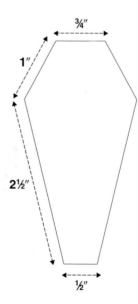

Coffin Cookies

Graveyard Treat

2¼ cups chocolate wafer
    cookie crumbs,
    divided
½ cup sugar, divided
½ cup (1 stick) margarine
    or butter, melted
1 package (8 ounces)
    PHILADELPHIA®
    Cream Cheese, cubed,
    softened
1 tub (12 ounces) COOL
    WHIP® Whipped
    Topping, thawed
2 cups boiling water
1 package (8-serving size)
    or 2 packages
    (4-serving size)
    JELL-O® Brand Orange
    Flavor Gelatin
½ cup cold water
    Ice cubes
    Rectangular or oval-
    shaped sandwich
    cookies
    Decorator icings
    Candy corn and
    pumpkins

MIX 2 cups of the cookie crumbs, ¼ cup of the sugar and the melted margarine with fork in 13×9-inch baking pan until crumbs are well moistened. Press firmly onto bottom of pan to form crust. Refrigerate.

BEAT cream cheese and remaining ¼ cup sugar in medium bowl with wire whisk until smooth. Gently stir in ½ of the whipped topping. Spread evenly over crust.

STIR boiling water into gelatin in medium bowl 2 minutes or until completely dissolved. Mix cold water and ice cubes to make 1½ cups. Add to gelatin; stir until slightly thickened (consistency of unbeaten egg whites). Remove any remaining ice. Spoon gelatin over cream cheese layer.

REFRIGERATE 3 hours or until firm. Spread remaining whipped topping over gelatin just before serving; sprinkle with remaining ¼ cup cookie crumbs. Decorate sandwich cookies with icings to make "tombstones." Stand tombstones on top of dessert with candies to resemble a graveyard. Cut into squares to serve. *Makes 15 to 18 servings*

Graveyard Treat

Orange Jack-O'-Lanterns

INGREDIENTS
6 oranges
1 package (5 ounces) cook-and-serve chocolate pudding mix
2¼ cups milk
1 cup mini semisweet chocolate chips
4 ounces cream cheese, softened and cut into ½-inch cubes
½ teaspoon orange extract
Green Cream Cheese Frosting (recipe follows)
Green Slivered Almonds (recipe follows)

SUPPLIES
Pastry bag with leaf tip

◆ Cut tops from oranges; discard tops. Scoop out fruit and membranes; reserve for another use or discard. With sharp knife, cut out jack-o'-lantern faces in sides of oranges.

◆ Combine pudding mix and milk in medium saucepan. Cook over medium-high heat, stirring constantly, until pudding comes to a boil. Remove saucepan from heat. Add chocolate chips, cream cheese and extract; stir until chips and cream cheese are melted. Cool.

◆ Spoon pudding mixture into oranges. Cover lightly with plastic wrap; refrigerate several hours or overnight.

◆ When ready to serve, spoon Green Cream Cheese Frosting into pastry bag fitted with leaf tip; pipe onto pudding for pumpkin leaves as shown in photo. Add almonds for stems, if desired. *Makes 6 servings*

Green Cream Cheese Frosting

4 ounces cream cheese, softened
2 tablespoons powdered sugar
Green food color

◆ Beat cream cheese and powdered sugar in small bowl until well blended. Color with green food color.
Makes about ½ cup

Green Slivered Almonds: Place 6 slivered almonds in small resealable plastic food storage bag. Add ⅛ teaspoon green food color; seal bag. Shake bag until almonds are evenly colored. Place almonds on paper-towel-lined plate; let dry.

Smucker's® Spider Web Tartlets

1 16-ounce log refrigerated sugar cookie dough
¾ cup flour
    Nonstick cooking spray or parchment paper
1 cup (12-ounce jar) SMUCKER'S® Apricot Preserves
1 tube black cake decorating gel

◆ Preheat the oven to 375°F. Unwrap cookie dough and place in medium mixing bowl. With floured hands, knead flour into cookie dough. Roll dough back into log shape, place on clean cutting board and cut into eight equal slices. With floured fingers, place dough circles onto baking sheet lined with parchment paper or sprayed with nonstick spray.

◆ Gently press dough circles, flattening to make each one approximately 4 inches in diameter. With thumb and forefinger, pinch the edge of each dough circle to create a ridge all around. Pinch each dough circle along the ridge to make eight points.

◆ Spread 2 tablespoons of Smucker's® Jam (or Simply Fruit) onto each dough circle, making sure to spread it all the way to the edges and in the points. Refrigerate for 20 minutes. Bake 12 to 14 minutes or until edges are lightly browned.

◆ Remove tartlets from baking sheet and cool on wire rack. When cool, use the black decorating gel to make a spider web design. *Makes 8 servings*

Haunted Hint

For a really eerie setting, replace regular light bulbs with black, strobe or colored light bulbs. Then arrange false cobwebs on and around the lamp shades to create some menacing shadows.

Yummy Mummy Cookies

⅔ cup butter or
    margarine, softened
1 cup sugar
2 teaspoons vanilla
    extract
2 eggs
2½ cups all-purpose flour
½ cup HERSHEY'S Cocoa
¼ teaspoon baking soda
½ teaspoon salt
1 cup HERSHEY'S MINI
    CHIPS™ Semi-Sweet
    Chocolate
1 to 2 packages
    (10 ounces each)
    HERSHEY'S Premier
    White Chips
1 to 2 tablespoons
    shortening (do not
    use butter, margarine,
    spread or oil)
    Additional HERSHEY'S
    MINI CHIPS™ Semi-
    Sweet Chocolate

1. Beat butter, sugar and vanilla in large bowl until creamy. Add eggs; beat well. Stir together flour, cocoa, baking soda and salt; gradually add to butter mixture, beating until blended. Stir in 1 cup small chocolate chips. Refrigerate dough 15 to 20 minutes or until firm enough to handle.

2. Heat oven to 350°F. To form mummy body, using 1 tablespoon dough, roll into 3½-inch carrot shape; place on ungreased cookie sheet. To form head, using 1 teaspoon dough, roll into ball the size and shape of a grape; press onto wide end of body. Repeat procedure with remaining dough. Bake 8 to 9 minutes or until set. Cool slightly; remove from cookie sheet to wire rack. Cool.

3. Place 1⅔ cups (10-ounce package) white chips and 1 tablespoon shortening in microwave-safe pie plate or shallow bowl. Microwave at HIGH (100%) 1 minute; stir until chips are melted.

4. Coat tops of cookies by placing one cookie at a time on table knife or narrow metal spatula; spoon white chip mixture evenly over cookie to coat. (If mixture begins to thicken, return to microwave for a few seconds). Place coated cookies on wax paper. Melt additional chips with shortening, if needed, for additional coating. As coating begins to set on cookies, using a toothpick, score lines and facial features into coating to resemble mummy. Place 2 small chocolate chips on each cookie for eyes. Store, covered, in cool, dry place.
Makes about 30 cookies

Macho Monster Cake

1 package (18.25 ounces) cake mix, any flavor, plus ingredients to prepare mix
1 container (16 ounces) cream cheese or vanilla frosting
Green and yellow food color
Black decorating gel
1 white chocolate baking bar (2 ounces)

SUPPLIES
1 (13×9-inch) cake board, covered, or large tray

◆ Preheat oven to 350°F. Lightly grease and flour 13×9-inch baking pan.

◆ Prepare cake mix according to package directions. Pour into prepared pan.

◆ Bake 30 to 35 minutes until toothpick inserted into center comes out clean. Cool in pan on wire rack 10 minutes. Remove to rack; cool completely.

◆ Tint frosting with green and yellow food color to make ugly monster green as shown in photo. If cake top is rounded, trim horizontally with long serrated knife. Using Diagram 1 as guide, draw pattern pieces on waxed paper. Cut pieces out and place on cake. Cut around patterns with knife. Remove and discard patterns.

◆ Position pieces on prepared cake board as shown in Diagram 2, connecting with some frosting. Frost cake. Using decorating gel, pipe eyes, mouth, hair and scars as shown. Break white chocolate baking bar into irregular pieces; position inside mouth as teeth.
Makes 12 servings

ꟼote: For cleaner cutting lines, place the cooled cake in the freezer for 30 to 45 minutes before cutting.

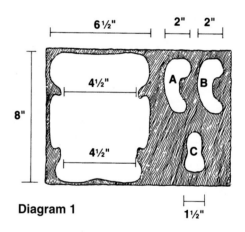

Diagram 1

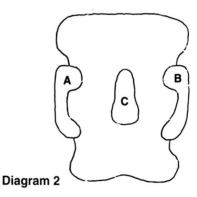

Diagram 2

Macho Monster Cake

Skeleton Cookies

30 to 40 drops black food coloring
1 package (about 18 ounces) refrigerated sugar cookie dough
All-purpose flour
Skeleton or gingerbread man cookie cutters
1 tube white frosting

◆ Knead food coloring into cookie dough on lightly floured waxed paper.* Wrap in plastic wrap and refrigerate 2 hours or until very firm.

◆ Preheat oven to 350°F.

◆ Roll out dough between floured sheets of waxed paper to ⅛-inch thickness. Cut dough with cookie cutters.

◆ Bake 9 to 13 minutes or until edges are firm (centers will be somewhat soft). Cool 1 minute on cookie sheet. Remove to wire rack; cool completely.

◆ Draw skeleton figures on cookies with frosting.

Makes about 2 dozen cookies

*Cookies will appear a shade or two lighter after baking. While kneading in the black food coloring, add a few more drops of coloring after the desired shade has been reached.

Set a creepy table for your party! For each guest, roll up a paper napkin and use a plastic spider ring as a napkin ring.

Skeleton Cookies

Halloween Haunted House

1 container (16 ounces) chocolate fudge frosting
Pretzel sticks, nuts, fudge-coated graham crackers, black licorice twists, black jelly beans, sugar wafers, candy corn, dried papaya, rice crackers, and other assorted candies

SUPPLIES
2 empty 1-quart milk cartons, rinsed and dried
1 (13×11-inch) cake board, covered, or large tray

◆ Tape each milk carton closed at top. Tape milk cartons together to make house; wrap with foil. Attach securely to covered cake board with tape.

◆ Frost cartons with chocolate frosting; decorate using frosting to attach decorations.

Makes 1 house

Chocolate Spiders

¼ cup butter
1 package (12 ounces) semisweet chocolate chips
1 cup butterscotch chips
¼ cup creamy peanut butter
4 cups crisp rice cereal
Chow mein noodles and assorted candies

◆ Cover baking sheet with waxed paper. Combine butter, chocolate chips and butterscotch chips in large saucepan; stir over medium heat until chips are melted and mixture is well blended. Remove from heat. Add peanut butter; mix well. Add cereal; stir to evenly coat.

◆ Drop mixture by tablespoonfuls onto prepared baking sheet; insert chow mein noodles for legs and add candies for eyes.   *Makes about 3 dozen*

Doughnut Hole Spiders: Substitute chocolate-covered doughnut holes for shaped cereal mixture. Insert black string licorice, cut into 1½-inch lengths, into doughnut holes for legs. Use decorating icing to dot onto doughnut holes for eyes.

Halloween Haunted House

Index

Acknowledgments

The publisher would like to thank the companies and organizations listed below for the use of their recipes and photographs in this publication.

Birds Eye®

Hershey Foods Corporation

Idaho Potato Commission

Kraft Foods, Inc.

Lipton®

Nabisco Biscuit Company

National Chicken Council

PLANTERS® Baking Nuts

The J.M. Smucker Company

Washington Apple Commission